T
OF THE MASS

by
Father Paul O'Sullivan, O.P.
(E.D.M.)

"For from the rising of the sun even to the going down, my name is great among the Gentiles, and in every place there is sacrifice, and there is offered to my name a clean oblation: for my name is great among the Gentiles, saith the Lord of hosts." —Malachias 1:11

TAN Books
Charlotte, North Carolina

With permission of the Superiors of the Order:
A.R.P. Fr. Louis C. Coffey, O.P.
Prior Provincial
Providence of Ireland
August 27, 1963

APPROVED BY HIS EMINENCE CARDINAL CEREJEIRA
CARDINAL PATRIARCH OF LISBON

First published *circa* 1963 by the former Edições do Corpo Santo, Lisbon, Portugal. Retypeset and republished in 1993 by TAN Books and Publishers, with permission of Saint Martin de Porres Apostolate, Dublin, Ireland.

ISBN: 978-0-89555-491-8

Library of Congress Catalog Card No.: 93-60344

Printed and bound in the United States of America.

TAN Books
Charlotte, North Carolina
2008

These beautiful pages on the Mass have been approved by:

His Eminence Cardinal Cerejeira

His Eminence Cardinal Pietro Ciriaci,
Papal Nuncio, Lisbon

His Grace the Archbishop of Braga

His Grace the Archbishop of Evora

His Grace the Archbishop of Aveiro

His Lordship the Bishop of Coimbra

His Lordship the Bishop of Beja

His Lordship the Bishop of Portalegre

BOOKS BY
FATHER PAUL O'SULLIVAN, O.P.

HOW TO BE HAPPY—HOW TO BE HOLY

ALL ABOUT THE ANGELS

AN EASY WAY TO BECOME A SAINT

THE HOLY GHOST—OUR GREATEST FRIEND

READ ME OR RUE IT

HOW TO AVOID PURGATORY

THE SECRET OF CONFESSION
Including The Wonders of Confession

THE WONDERS OF THE HOLY NAME

THE WONDERS OF THE MASS

ST. PHILOMENA—THE WONDER-WORKER

Contents

Chapter 1

The Wonders of Holy Mass

The Saints never speak so eloquently as when they speak of the Mass. They can never say enough on this sublime subject, for St. Bonaventure says that the wonders of the Mass are as many as there are stars in the heavens and grains of sand on the seashores of the world.

The graces, blessings and favors granted to those who assist at this Divine Sacrifice are beyond all comprehension.

The Mass is the greatest wonder in the world. There is nothing on Earth equal to it, and there is nothing in Heaven greater than it.

The next greatest wonder is the indifference and ignorance of Catholics regarding Holy Mass. How is it that so many Catholics do not go to Mass?

The Great Sacrifice of Calvary is offered near to their homes, almost at their very doors, and they are too slothful to assist at it.

The Sacrifice of Calvary?! Yes, for the Mass is really and truly the very same as the Death of Jesus on the Cross. [See footnote on p. 8.]

Why do not mothers, why do not catechists, why do not teachers instill into the minds and hearts of

those in their charge the wonders of the Mass?
Priests are bound by the Council of Trent to do so.

Protestants may well ask those Catholics who
neglect hearing daily Mass *if they do really believe*
that God is born on the altar and that God dies on
the altar as He did on Calvary? [See footnote on p.
8.] If they do believe, why do they not assist at Mass?

St. Augustine tells us that pagans and Gentiles
of his time asked tepid and indifferent Christians
with bitter irony if they sincerely believed that the
God of all mercy and goodness descended on their
altars! You Christians, they continued, accuse us of
adoring false gods, but at least we believe they are
gods and we honor them; whereas, you despise Him
whom you call the True God!

No intelligent, no enlightened Christian would
fail to attend Mass if he only knew what it was.

St. Louis and the Mass

King Louis of France, who labored perhaps more
strenuously than any man in his kingdom and who
was one of the best and most glorious sovereigns
who ever ruled over France, found time to hear two
or three Masses every day!

Some of his courtiers suggested that he was over-
taxing himself with so many Masses. The King
replied: "If I spent much more time in following
the pleasures of the chase, or in entertaining my

friends at rich banquets, or in frequenting for several hours each day theaters and places of amusement, you would not complain that I was devoting too much time to pleasure.

"You forget, my good friends, that by hearing Mass I not only secure for myself innumerable blessings, but I confer the most important benefits on my kingdom, many more than I could possibly do in any other way."

This reply of St. Louis may be addressed to those thousands and thousands of apathetic and indifferent Christians who could easily hear daily Mass and do not do so.

Even were they to make a great sacrifice, they would receive blessings and favors above their highest hopes. But, as a matter of fact, many could hear Mass without any sacrifice, or at so trifling a cost that their guilt in neglecting this Divine Sacrifice is, indeed, incomprehensible. Nothing but lamentable ignorance can explain the reason why so many Catholics neglect to hear daily Mass.

By hearing Mass, the day would become worth a thousand days to them, so wonderful would be the graces and benefits they should receive.

Far from losing time, their business would prosper more, and they would reach a degree of happiness that they could never otherwise hope to attain.

Simon De Montfort

The famous general and hero, Simon de Mont-
fort, with only 800 horse soldiers and very few foot
soldiers, was unexpectedly trapped in the town of
Muret by an army of 40,000 men led by the King
of Aragon and Raymond the Count of Toulouse, who
espoused the cause of the Albigensian heretics. He
was hearing Mass when his officers came to
announce that the besieging army was marching to
attack the town.

"Let me first finish Mass," he replied, "and then
I will be with you."

He then hastened to where his forces were already
gathered together, bade them trust in God, and order-
ing the gates to be flung open, he charged right at
the heart of the approaching army, threw it into utter
disorder, struck down the King of Aragon himself
and won a glorious victory.

Baronius declares that the **Emperor Lothaire**
heard three Masses every day, even when he was
on the battlefield with his troops.

In the Great War [World War I] it was well known
that Marshal Foch, the Commander-in-chief of the
French and British armies, heard Mass every day,
even when the position was most critical.

The Emperor Otho of Germany once summoned
a council of his chief officers and advisers to take

place in the Palace at Worms, at an early hour in the morning.

The Duke of Bohemia, one of the princes who was to take part in the council, was wont to hear Mass daily and was, therefore, late in arriving at the royal palace.

This delay threw the Emperor into a fury, and without waiting for the Duke, he commenced the council, giving orders to all present not to show honor or give any greeting to the Duke on his arrival.

Some short time after, the Duke entered the council chamber and to the surprise of those present, the Emperor, who at first seemed startled, rose in haste and showed every mark of respect to the Duke. When the weighty matters of state had been discussed, the Emperor Otho, noticing the surprise manifested by the assembled lords and princes at his change of demeanor toward the Duke of Bohemia, explained: "Why," he said, "did you not see that he came accompanied by two angels, one on either side? I dared not show my resentment."

Similar wonderful favors are granted to the humblest of the faithful, to anyone who hears Mass devoutly.

Here are some incidents.

The Angel and the Roses

A poor farmer was wont to attend daily Mass for many years of his life.

He was crossing the snow-covered fields one cold morning on his way to church. He thought that he heard footsteps behind him, and turning, he saw his Angel Guardian bearing a basket full of beautiful roses, which exhaled a delicious perfume. "See," said the Angel, "these roses represent each step you have taken on the way to Mass, and each rose represents, too, a glorious reward which awaits you in Heaven. But far, far greater are the merits you have gotten from the Mass itself."

How to Make One's Business Prosper

Two businessmen resided in the same French town. Both were engaged in the same line of commerce, but while one was prosperous, the other found it very hard to gain a sufficiency, notwithstanding that he worked harder and rose earlier than his friend.

Reduced to extremities, he resolved to seek advice from his prosperous colleague, hoping to learn the secret of his success.

"My good friend," replied the wealthy merchant, "I have no secrets, I work just as you work. If there is any difference in our methods, it is this: I go to

Mass daily. You do not. Follow my sincere advice, hear Mass every morning, and I feel sure that God will bless your work."

The poorer man did as he was advised, and soon, in some unaccountable way, his difficulties ceased and his business prospered beyond all his expectations.

Chapter 2

What Is the Mass?

1. In the Mass the Son of God becomes man again, so that in every Mass the stupendous Mystery of the Incarnation, with all its infinite merits, is repeated as truly as when the Son of God first took flesh in the womb of the Virgin Mary.

St. Augustine: "What a sublime dignity is that of the priest, in whose hands Christ once more becomes man!"

2. The Mass is the birth of Jesus Christ. He is really born on the Altar each time that Mass is said, as He was born in Bethlehem.

St. John Damascene: "If anyone wishes to know how the bread is changed into the Body of Jesus Christ, I will tell him. The Holy Ghost overshadows the priest and acts on him as He acted on the Blessed Virgin Mary."

---

* The statements that Jesus (God) "dies" in the Mass and that the Blood of Jesus "is shed" in the Mass refer to an *unbloody* and *mystical* renewal of His death and blood-shedding, since, as regards physical death, "Christ rising again from the dead, dieth now no more, death shall no more have dominion over him." (*Rom.* 6:9). See also *The Hidden Treasure: Holy Mass* by St. Leonard of Port Maurice, p. 22, and *The Incredible Catholic Mass*, by Fr. Martin von Cochem, chaps. 9 and 10. —*Publisher*, 2004.

St. Bonaventure: "God, when He descends upon the altar, does no less than He did when He became man the first time in the womb of the Virgin Mary."

3. The Mass is the same as the Sacrifice of Calvary. In it God dies* as He died on the first Good Friday. It has the same infinite value of Calvary, and brings down on men the same priceless graces.

The Mass is not an imitation, or a memory of Calvary, it is **identically the same Sacrifice** and differs from Calvary only in the manner of offering.

In every Mass the Blood of Jesus is shed for us again. [See footnote on p. 8.]

St. Augustine: "In the Mass the Blood of Christ flows anew for sinners."

4. Nothing on this Earth, nothing in Heaven itself, gives more glory to God and obtains more benefits for us than a single Mass.

5. By the Mass we offer to God the greatest praise, the greatest glory He could possibly desire. We give Him most perfect thanks for all the benefits He has bestowed on us. We make more reparation for our faults than by the severest penances.

6. We can do nothing better for the conversion of sinners than offer for them the Holy Sacrifice of the Mass. If mothers would only hear and get Masses said for their erring children, and wives for their husbands, how happy their families would be!

7. No prayers, no suffrages, no matter how

fervent, can help the Holy Souls as the Mass. Oh, let us think of the Souls in Purgatory! Among them may be our dear father and mother and friends. We can help them most easily, we can relieve their awful pains most efficaciously by hearing Mass for them.

What the Saints Say of the Mass

To make still more manifest what we have just stated, we shall quote the very words of the Saints and holy Doctors.

St. Lawrence Justinian: "There is no prayer or good work so great, so pleasing to God, so useful to us as the Mass."

St. Alphonsus: "Even God Himself could do nothing holier, better, or greater than the Mass."

St. Thomas teaches that the Mass is nothing less than the Sacrifice of Calvary renewed on the altar, and that every Mass brings to men the same benefits as the Sacrifice of the Cross.

St. John Chrysostom: "The Mass has just the same value as Calvary."

St. Bonaventure: "The Mass is a compendium of all God's love, of all His benefits to men, and each Mass bestows on the World a benefit not less than what was conferred on it by the Incarnation."

St. Hanon, Bishop of Cologne, once saw a globe of extraordinary beauty and brilliancy circle round the Chalice at the Consecration and then enter the sacred vessel. He was so filled with awe that he feared to go on with the Mass, but God revealed to him that this happened at every Mass, though not visible to our human eyes.

The Host is nothing else than the great Eternal, Omnipotent God who fills Heaven with His Majesty. Why do we not realize it?

St. Odo of Cluny: "The happiness of the World comes from the Sacrifice of the Mass."

Timothy of Jerusalem: "The World would have been destroyed long ago because of the sins of men, had it not been for the Mass."

"There is nothing that appeases the anger of God so much, nothing that obtains for us so many blessings as the Mass."

St. Lawrence Justinian: "No human tongue can describe the immense favors and blessings which we receive from the Mass. The sinner obtains pardon, the good man becomes more holy, our faults are corrected and our vices uprooted by hearing Holy Mass."

Fornerius: "By one Mass which we hear in the state of grace, we give God more pleasure and obtain for ourselves more benefits and favors than by the longest and most painful pilgrimages."

Marchant: "If we were to offer to the Holy Trinity all the penances, all the prayers, all the good works of all the Saints, if we were to offer the torrents of blood, all the sufferings of the twelve Apostles and the millions of martyrs, all would give Him less glory and pleasure than one Mass! Why? Because the Mass is truly and really the Sacrifice of Mount Calvary. In the Mass, Jesus Christ offers to His Eternal Father all the pains, humiliations and infinite merits of His Passion and Death."

The Mass obtains for us the very greatest graces, blessings and favors, spiritual and temporal—graces that we could not possibly receive in any other way.

It saves us from countless dangers and delivers us from the evils that threaten us.

St. Alphonsus asks: What is the reason for all this?

He answers that the Mass is infinite in value; whereas, all the prayers and good works of the Angels and Saints, though of exceeding great merit and though they give unspeakable glory to God, yet are finite and therefore bear no comparison with the infinite Sacrifice of the Mass.

Just as all creation, the heavens and the earth, the sun, the moon and the stars, the mountains and oceans, all men and angels are nothing in comparison with God, so no good works, however holy, are equal to one Mass. The Mass is God Himself.

The Angels and the Mass

St. Gregory: "The Heavens open and multitudes of Angels come to assist at the Holy Sacrifice."

St. Augustine: "The Angels surround and help the priest when he is celebrating Mass."

St. John Chrysostom: "When Mass is being celebrated, the Sanctuary is filled with countless Angels, who adore the Divine Victim immolated on the altar."

The efficacy of the Mass is so wonderful, God's mercy and generosity are then so unlimited, that there is no moment so propitious to ask for favors as when Jesus is born on the altar. What we then ask we shall almost certainly receive, and what we do not obtain in the Mass we may scarcely hope to receive by all other prayers, penances or pilgrimages.

The Angels know this full well and come in multitudes to adore God and make their petitions at this hour of mercy.

We read in the revelations of St. Bridget: "One day when I was assisting at the Holy Sacrifice, I saw an immense number of Holy Angels descend and gather around the altar, contemplating the priest. They sang heavenly canticles that ravished my heart; Heaven itself seemed to be contemplating the great Sacrifice. And yet we poor, blind and miserable creatures assist at the Mass with so little love, relish and respect!

"Oh, if God would open our eyes, what wonders should we not see!"

When Blessed Henry Suso, the holy Dominican,

was saying Mass, Angels in visible form gathered around the altar, and some came near to him in raptures of love.

This is what takes place at every Mass, though we do not see it.

Do Catholics ever think of this amazing truth? At Mass they are praying in the midst of thousands of God's Angels.

Chapter 3

The Joy of the Saints at Mass

St. Dominic was accustomed to pass the night in prayer before the Blessed Sacrament. In the morning he celebrated Mass with the fervor of a seraph, and he was sometimes so filled with love and delight that his body was raised in the air and his face shone with a supernatural light.

St. John of the Cross said Mass with extraordinary love and devotion.

Once, having pronounced the words of Consecration, his face shone with such a brilliant light that many of those in the church gathered around the altar to gaze at the wonderful brightness.

After Mass, the Superior begged him to say what had happened, and he replied: "At the Consecration, God revealed Himself to me in such majesty and glory that I feared that I could not continue the Mass."

Blessed John of Alverne said Mass with a like devotion. On the feast of the Assumption his soul was so filled with holy fear and emotion that he tried in vain to pronounce the words of Consecration. He began and paused; he began again and paused again. His Superior, remarking his trouble, helped him to say the whole form.

Scarcely had Blessed John finished the words than he saw the Sacred Host take the form of the Divine Child, and he was so overcome that only with the help of two priests was he able to conclude the Holy Sacrifice.

He then fainted away in an ecstasy of love.

Thomas of Cantimbre, the celebrated Dominican Bishop, who was famed for his profound learning and deep piety, describes a miracle which he himself witnessed in company with many others.

Having heard that Our Blessed Lord had appeared visibly in a Consecrated Host in the Church of St. Amand, in Douay, he hastened thither and begged the priest to open the tabernacle and expose the sacred Particle. Many persons had flocked to the Church on learning of the Bishop's arrival and were privileged to see once more Our Divine Lord.

The Bishop tells us what he himself saw: "I saw my Lord face to face. His eyes were clear and had an expression of wondrous love. His hair was abundant and floated on His shoulders. His beard was long, His forehead broad and high, His cheeks were pale and His head slightly inclined. At the sight of my loving Lord, my heart well nigh burst with joy and love.

"After a little time Our Lord's face assumed an expression of profound sadness, such as it must have worn in the Passion. He was crowned with thorns, and His face bathed in blood.

"On looking at the countenance of my Sweet Saviour thus changed, my heart was pierced with bitter grief, tears flowed from my eyes, and I seemed to feel the points of the thorns enter my head."

St. John of the Augustinian Order was consumed with such a love for the Mass that he was accustomed to rise early in the morning in order to satisfy his eager desire to celebrate the Holy Sacrifice as soon as possible. His devotion was, indeed, admirable and his soul was filled with rapture, especially at the moment of Consecration.

Those who served his Mass, however, complained to the Superior that the good Father wearied them by the extraordinary length of time he took to say his Mass, which prevented them from fulfilling their other duties. The Superior charged him to finish his Mass more speedily, like the other members of the community.

The good priest obeyed these instructions, but at the end of some days, he threw himself at the feet of the prior and implored him to be allowed to devote more time to the celebration of Holy Mass.

Urged by the Superior to state his reasons for this unusual devotion, Father John revealed to him the divine favors he received, and how he visibly saw Jesus Christ on the altar, adding details that filled the prior with such great fear and emotions as almost made him faint.

The narration of these facts gave the Superior a new and ardent fervor at Holy Mass during the remainder of his life.

St. Raymond of Peñafort, Superior General of the Dominican Order, said Mass with angelic fervor. On one occasion, a globe of fire covered his head and shoulders, like a glorious aureola, from the Consecration to the Communion of the Mass.

Blessed Francis of Possadas of the same Order was no less favored. His face shone with an extraordinary splendor and became beautiful in the extreme, as if he received a new life. One day a flame of brilliant light issued from his mouth and lit up the Missal when he was reading the Gospel. On two occasions during the Feast of Pentecost, a similar splendor emanated from his whole body and illuminated the altar.

When he was pronouncing the words of Consecration, Our Lord said to him with infinite love: "My son, I AM WHO AM." After consuming the Host, Blessed Francis was raised up and remained suspended in the air.

St. Ignatius was wont to say Mass with rapt devotion. One day the assistant saw a bright flame circle around his head and hastened to extinguish it, when lo, he discovered that it was a supernatural radiance that enveloped the head of the Saint!

Blessed Francis of the Order of Minors suffered for many years from grievous pains in the legs so that any movement caused him intense suffering.

But his devotion to the Mass was so great that during all these years, full of faith, he arose from his couch in the morning and celebrated the Divine Mysteries without the slightest inconvenience.

Blessed John, a Dominican of Ravenna, was frequently seen enveloped in a heavenly splendor during Mass.

The lives of the Saints are full of similar marvels. What we must bear in mind, however, is that in every Mass we hear, no matter how humble the priest may be, the Mysteries are the same, infinite in number, as St. Bonaventure says. It is the same Infinite, Omnipotent, Eternal God who is born on the altar and who offers Himself as truly as He did on Calvary, for those who assist at Mass.

Chapter 4

Priests, the Happiest of Men

Not only the Saints but all devout priests experience the most profound satisfaction and joy when celebrating Mass. It is enough for them to know

1. That they are in immediate, intimate, personal communication with God Himself; that they are holding Him in their hands, looking at Him, conversing with Him and that He is looking into their very hearts with ineffable love.

2. That they are giving Him the greatest possible joy and glory that even He could desire, greater glory than all the Angels and Saints give Him in Heaven.

3. That they are calling down on themselves, on the World, on their native land countless blessings.

4. That they are surrounded by throngs of Holy Angels who are watching their every movement.

5. Finally, that they are helping, consoling, rejoicing the Holy Souls in Purgatory.

How is it possible for a devout and intelligent priest to know and feel all this and not be filled with joy?

The Mass of Leo XIII

"I was once admitted to assist at the Mass of Pope Leo XIII," a venerable priest told us, "and no book that I ever read on the Mass, no sermon I ever heard produced on me such a profound impression.

"It is not fifty years since that happy day, and never since have I forgotten that Mass of the Holy Father. Never have I celebrated Mass myself that I have not tried to imitate the devotion he manifested at his Mass.

"The Pope was then eighty-five years of age, and seemed to me feeble and considerably bent as he entered the chapel. When, however, he proceeded to the altar, he was filled with a new life, a new energy.

"He began the Holy Sacrifice absorbed in devotion. All his gestures, all his movements, his slow, distinct utterance of the words showed clearly that he felt that he was in the very presence of God. At the moment of Consecration, his face lit up with a beautiful light, his great eyes shone and his whole expression was as of one looking at, conversing with the Almighty.

"He took the Host in his hands with the utmost reverence and pronounced the solemn words of Consecration, manifestly with a full comprehension of the tremendous act he was performing.

"He then bent his knee as if before the throne of God in Heaven, he raised the Host aloft and gazed at it in rapture, slowly returning it to the corporal.

"He manifested the same unction and living faith at the Consecration of the most Precious Blood.

"Thence on to the Communion, his fervor was visible at every moment.

"At the **Agnus Dei** he seemed to be speaking face to face with God.

"I do not venture to describe with what love he consumed the Sacred Host and drank the Precious Blood of Jesus.

"And yet the Mass was not very long, the whole ceremony was simple, but so impressive that, as I have said, it has been ever before my eyes for fifty long years."

A Protestant Converted by the Mass

A group of English tourists, Protestants, assisted at the Holy Sacrifice in the Cathedral Church of Florence. The celebrant said the Mass with deep devotion, quite unaware that he was being closely watched by this group of strangers. Some of the group, when their curiosity had been satisfied, left their places near the altar and proceeded to examine the beauties of the sacred edifice. One, however, remained behind and continued to watch every movement of the priest until the conclusion of the Holy Sacrifice.

He was evidently profoundly moved and was

especially struck by the look of faith and joy visible on the priest's face as he came from the altar and proceeded to the sacristy. On his return to England, this gentleman begged for instruction and became a fervent Catholic.

We do not hesitate to say that, when Protestants or unbelievers assist at a Mass said devoutly, they are frequently so deeply impressed that many of them, like the Englishman whom we have just mentioned, enter the Church.

Hasty and Irreverent Masses

Far different, says St. Alphonsus, are the sad results caused to those who assist at a Mass hastily and irreverently celebrated.

Father Mateo Crawley

Father Mateo Crawley was, without doubt, one of the greatest missionaries in the world. Yet there was no one more kind, more modest, more winning. Even when speaking of the greatest sinners whom it had been his lot to encounter, he referred to them with kindness and pity.

Yet one fact he recounts with great sadness. We heard the story from his own lips. "My father," he said, "was a Protestant, a good-living, honest, straightforward man. My mother was a Catholic and reared her children in the Catholic Faith. Her most ardent desire was to see my father converted. She acted with great tact and prudence. She placed her hope rather in prayer and example than in persuasion, though she found means, too, of making known to my father, without annoying him, the truths of the Catholic Church.

"At last her hopes were on the verge of being fulfilled, so much so, that my father promised to come with us to Mass.

"He did so, but unfortunately the priest celebrated the Mass with so much haste and irreverence that my father returned home disappointed and declared that never, never more, would he think of becoming a Catholic.

"We, too, were profoundly disappointed, all the more as my father refused to listen to any further reference to the Catholic Faith. Years passed and we continued to pray.

"One evening a missionary priest of the Passionist Order called on us, and my father in his usual hospitable manner invited him to remain.

"By a strange providence the conversation of this missionary produced a striking effect on my father! Once more he consented to hear Mass, to be celebrated by the missionary.

"The Passionist Father celebrated Mass very simply but very piously, and thanks to Almighty God, my good father shortly after began a course of instruction and entered the Church."

Chapter 5

The Benefits of the Mass

St. Thomas, the Prince of Theologians, writes wonderfully of the Mass.

"The Mass," he says, "obtains for sinners in mortal sin the grace of repentance. For the just, it obtains the remission of venial sins and the pardon of the pain due to sin. It obtains an increase of habitual [Sanctifying] grace, as well as all the graces necessary for their special needs."

St. Paul, the Hermit, stood once at the church door as the people entered. He saw the soul of one man, a great sinner, in such a state of horrible corruption as appalled him. Moreover, he saw a devil standing by his side who seemed to have complete control of him. On leaving the church, he saw the same man so completely changed that he called him aside and asked him confidentially if he was sorry for his sins. The poor man at once confessed that he had committed many and very grave sins, but during the Mass he had read in his prayer book, "If your sins are as red as scarlet, I will make them as white as snow." "I began at once to ask God to pardon and forgive me, and I am very sorry for my sins and I wish to go to Confession at once."

St. Paul saw that by his act of sincere sorrow the man was, by the infinite merits of the Mass, pardoned of all his sins.

Our Lord said to St. Mechtilde: "In Mass I come with such humility that there is no sinner, no matter how depraved he be, that I am not ready to receive, if only he desires it. I come with such sweetness and mercy that I will pardon my greatest enemies, if they ask for pardon. I come with such generosity that there is no one so poor that I will not fill him with the riches of my love. I come with such heavenly food as will strengthen the weakest, with such light as will illumine the blindest, with such a plenitude of graces as will remove all miseries, overcome all obstinacy and dissipate all fears."

What words of divine comfort—words of God Himself! If we heard nothing else about the Holy Sacrifice of the Mass, are not these words alone sufficient to fill us with faith and confidence in the Divine Mysteries.

St. Gregory of Nazianzen. In the life of this great Saint we read that his father fell dangerously ill and was dying. The sick man had fallen into a state of such extreme weakness that he could scarcely make the slightest movement. His pulse was extremely weak, and he was not able to take any nourishment. At last he completely lost consciousness.

His family, despairing of all human means, placed their faith in God. They adjourned to the church, where Mass was said for the recovery of the sick man.

On their return, all danger had passed, and the patient was soon perfectly restored to health.

The Holy Curé of Ars fell grievously ill and, notwithstanding the constant help of doctors, grew rapidly worse, so that no hope was entertained of his life.

He asked that a Mass be said on the Altar of St. Philomena. At the conclusion of the Mass, he was completely cured.

In the city of Lisbon a lady lay dying of a mortal illness. The physicians held out no hope of recovery. She was suffering from a malignant cancer which had reached such extremes that an operation was impossible.

Her confessor suggested that a Mass should be offered for her complete cure.

The dying lady gladly accepted the counsel. The Mass was offered in honor of St. Dominic, and by its infinite efficacy the sick lady made a speedy recovery, much to the joy of her friends and to the surprise of her medical advisers.

How often do we not see in Christian homes the parents, the brothers, or the sisters ill unto death. Eminent physicians are summoned, costly remedies

are purchased, no pains are spared to save the dear
ones from death and hasten their recovery.

All that is as it should be, but **why forget, why
neglect** the most potent of all remedies, the Holy Mass?

How many men and women who are now lying
in their graves might be alive and well had Masses
been offered for them, as for the lady in Lisbon?

How many misfortunes and accidents would be
avoided if men had faith and confidence in the infinite merits of the Holy Sacrifice?

If Catholics only understood the efficacy of the
Mass, the churches would not be sufficient to hold
the multitudes that would flock to assist at the celebration of the Divine Mysteries.

Would to God that Christian mothers assisted at
and offered Masses for their families and, still better, if they trained their dear ones, from their youth
up, to assist at Holy Mass.

The Mass Obtains for Us a Happy Death

The crowning grace of our life is a holy and happy
death. What avails it to have had a long and happy
life, to have enjoyed all the comforts which riches
can give, all the honors the World can bestow, if in
the end we die a bad death?

An unhappy death means a never-ending eternity
of misery and woe.

We can only die once, and if we die badly, there

is no possibility of remedying the mistake. A bad death plunges a man into the fires of Hell forever and forever.

It is consequently of the utmost importance that we do all in our power, that we use every means possible to secure a happy death.

Holy writers recommend various excellent methods whereby we may make our salvation certain, and all these we should use to the best of our ability. All agree, however, that the best and easiest of these means is the frequent assistance at Holy Mass.

Our Blessed Lord assured St. Mechtilde that He would comfort and console all those who were assiduous in hearing Mass and that He would send as many of His great Saints to assist them when dying as they had heard Masses in their lifetime.

Penellas relates that a devout man had such confidence in the efficacy of the Mass that he did his utmost to be present at the Holy Sacrifice as often as he possibly could. He fell gravely ill and died with great peace and joy. His parish priest grieved much at the loss of this exemplary member of his flock and offered for his soul many suffrages.

Great was the surprise of the good priest when the dead man appeared to him radiant with joy and thanked him for his charity, adding at the same time that he was in no need of prayers, as owing to his frequent assistance at Mass, he was received immediately into Heaven.

Mgr. Nautier, Bishop of Breslau, notwithstanding his onerous labors and grave responsibilities, sought to be present at as many Masses as he could which were celebrated in his Cathedral.

At the moment of his death, his soul was seen mounting up to Heaven accompanied by many glorious Angels who sang sweet canticles of joy and praise.

All good Christians would do well to follow these holy examples and ask God every time they hear Mass to grant them the grace of a holy death and freedom from the fires of Purgatory.

Do Not Miss Mass

The obligation to hear Mass on Sundays and holy days is very grave and to fail in the fulfillment of this duty on these days, without sufficient reason, is a mortal sin. Not only does the sinner thereby lose important graces, which he may never again receive, but God may also punish him severely, as has frequently happened.

The following are some of the many instances we might mention.

The following fact happened near Rome. Three businessmen went to a fair at Cisterno, and after having transacted satisfactorily their business, two of them prepared to return home on Sunday morning. The third pointed out to them that they could not thus hear Mass. They laughed at his words and replied that they could go to Mass some other day. So saying, they mounted their horses and set out on their return journey.

Their companion heard Mass and then proceeded to follow them. What was not his consternation on learning that both his friends had been killed on the road, victims of a dreadful accident!

The writers of these lines remembers another awful punishment meted out by the Almighty to an unfortunate man in Rome itself. This man was a stone mason, and instead of hearing Mass on Sundays, he worked publicly, thereby giving no little scandal.

On the feast of Pentecost, he was engaged as usual at his sinful work on a high scaffolding when, lo, he was precipitated to the ground and killed instantly!

St. Antoninus of Florence quotes another instance of untimely death as a penalty for not hearing Mass.

Two young men went off together to hunt. One had heard Mass, the other had not. A storm of thunder and lightning suddenly burst over them. One, the unfortunate man who had not gone to Mass, was struck dead by the lightning; whereas, his companion escaped unscathed.

One of the principal duties of the Christian is to hear Mass on Sundays, the one day in the week consecrated to God. It is, indeed, very temerarious to neglect this obligation.

How a Poor Boy Became a Bishop, A Cardinal and a Saint

Peter Damian lost both father and mother shortly after his birth. One of his brothers adopted him, but treated him with unnatural harshness, forcing him to work hard and giving him poor food and scanty clothing.

One day, Peter found a silver piece which represented to him a small fortune. A friend told him that he could conscientiously use it for himself as the owner could not be found.

The only difficulty Peter had was to choose what it was he most needed, for he was in sore need of many things.

While turning the matter over in his young mind, it struck him that he could do a still better thing, viz., have a Mass said for the Holy Souls in Purgatory, especially for the souls of his dear parents. At the cost of a great sacrifice, he put this thought into effect and had the Mass offered.

A complete change at once became noticeable in his fortunes.

His eldest brother called at the house where he lived and, horrified at the brutal hardships the little fellow was subjected to, arranged that he be handed over to his own care. He clad him and fed him as his own child, educated and cared for him most affectionately. Blessing followed on blessing. Peter's wonderful talents became known, and he was rapidly promoted to the priesthood; some time after, he was raised to the episcopacy and finally created a Cardinal . . . Miracles attested his great sanctity so that after death he was canonized and declared a Doctor of the Church. These wonderful graces flowed, as from a fount, from that one Mass.

Chapter 6

Priests—Angels on Earth

If we understand the divine dignity of the priesthood, we shall comprehend more fully the infinite greatness of the Mass.

St. Ignatius Martyr says that the priesthood is the most sublime of all created dignities.

St. Ephrem calls it an infinite dignity.

Cassian says that the priest of God is exalted above all earthly sovereignties and above all celestial heights. He is inferior to God alone.

Pope Innocent III says that the priest is placed between God and man; inferior to God, but superior to man.

St. Denis calls the priest a divine man and the priesthood a divine dignity.

St. Ephrem says that the gift of the sacerdotal dignity surpasses all understanding.

Hence, **St. John Chrysostom** says that he who honors a priest honors Christ, and he who insults a priest, insults Christ.

St. Ambrose has called the priestly office a divine profession.

St. Francis de Sales, after having given orders to a holy ecclesiastic, perceived that in going out he

34

stopped at the door as if to give precedence to another. Being asked by the Saint why he stopped, he replied that God favored him with the visible presence of his Angel Guardian, who before he had received the priesthood always remained on his right and preceded him, but now since the moment of Ordination walked on his left and refused to go before him. It was in a holy contest with the Angel that he stopped at the door.

According to **St. Thomas,** the dignity of the priesthood surpasses even that of the angels.

St. Gregory Nazianzen has said that the angels themselves venerate the priesthood.

All the Angels in Heaven cannot absolve from a single sin. The Angel Guardians procure for the souls committed to their care grace to have recourse to a priest, that he may absolve them.

St. Francis of Assisi used to say: If I saw an angel and a priest, I would bend my knee first to the priest and then to the angel.

St. Augustine says that to pardon a sinner is a greater work than to create Heaven and Earth.

To pardon a single sin requires all the omnipotence of God. See the power of the priest.

St. Alphonsus: The entire Church cannot give God as much honor, or obtain so many graces as a single priest by celebrating a single Mass. Thus, by the celebration of a single Mass, in which he offers Jesus Christ in sacrifice, a priest gives greater honor to the Lord than if all men, by dying for God, offered Him the sacrifice of their lives.

With regard to the power of priests over the real body of Jesus Christ, it is of faith that when they pronounce the words of Consecration, the Incarnate Word has obliged Himself to obey and to come into their hands under the sacramental species.

St. Ignatius Martyr: Priests are the glory and the pillars of the Church, the doors and doorkeepers of Heaven.

St. Alphonsus: Were the Redeemer to descend into a Church and sit in a confessional, and a priest to sit in another confessional, Jesus would say over each penitent: "*Ego te absolvo.*" The priest would likewise say over each of his penitents: "*Ego te absolvo,*" and the penitents of each would be equally absolved. Thus, the sacerdotal dignity is the most noble of all the dignities in this world.

St. Ambrose says that it transcends all the dignities of kings, of emperors, and of angels. The dignity of the priest as far exceeds that of kings as the value of gold surpasses that of lead.

St. Cyprian said that all who had the true spirit of God were, when compelled to take the Order of priesthood, seized with fear and trembling.

St. Epiphanius writes that he found no one willing to be ordained a priest, so fearful were they of so divine a dignity.

St. Gregory Nazianzen says, in his life of St.

Cyprian, that when the Saint heard that his Bishop intended to ordain him a priest, he, through humility, concealed himself. It is related in the life of St. Fulgentius that he too fled away and hid himself.

St. Ambrose, as he himself attests, resisted for a long time before he consented to be ordained.

St. Francis of Assisi never consented to be ordained.

God Rewards Those Who Help Priests

A humble shopkeeper lived in a small town in Ireland with his wife and son. They had very little of this world's goods, but they were devout and went to Mass as often as they could.

A young priest, through ill health and over-study, lost his mental balance and was unable to perform his priestly duties. He wandered from place to place, gentle and sweet, giving no one trouble.

The good shopkeeper proposed to his wife to give him a little room in their modest house and give him food. The priest gladly accepted their kind invitation and spent some years with them, going and coming at his will.

Before death he regained the use of his reason and, sitting up in his deathbed, called on God most fervently to bless abundantly these good people: "Give them, dear Lord, a thousandfold for all they have given me, Your priest. Bless them spiritually and bless them temporally." So saying, he died.

Wonderful to say, that modest shopkeeper grew in wealth and prosperity, so that his son became a millionaire, and four of his sisters became nuns and four of his wife's sisters became nuns. He himself lived to a ripe old age.

Those who contribute generously to the education of students for the priesthood receive great rewards, for they could not possibly do anything greater than offer a good priest to God.

No one on this Earth can give God as much glory as a devout priest.

Chapter 7

How to Hear
Mass with Profit

1. The first condition for hearing Mass well is to understand thoroughly the infinite sanctity of the Holy Sacrifice and the graces it obtains.

To this end we must read, not once, but many times, this little book on the Mass.

The Mass, as we have seen, is a stupendous mystery. Our minds on the other hand are weak and slow to understand. Therefore, we must read frequently and ponder seriously on the wonders of the Mass. One Mass heard with understanding and devotion obtains for us more graces than a hundred, than a thousand Masses heard carelessly and in ignorance of what the Mass is.

2. We should make it an inviolable rule to arrive at church some minutes before Mass commences, firstly, in order to be prepared and recollected when the priest comes on the altar, and secondly, to avoid causing distraction to others.

3. We should not only hear Mass, but we should *offer* it with the priest. Moreover, we should have the

intention of hearing and offering all the Masses being said at the same time all over the world. In this way we receive a share in these innumerable Masses!

The Cross

4. We at once notice that the Crucifix is on every altar, that the priest's vestments are all marked with the Sign of the Cross, that the priest commences the Mass with the Sign of the Cross, that he makes this holy Sign very many times during the Mass. Why? To make clear to us that the Mass is really and truly the Sacrifice of the Cross, that in the Mass Christ is crucified, sheds His Precious Blood and dies for us. [See footnote on p. 8.] We must have no doubt that **we are really assisting at the Sacrifice of the Cross.**

Prayers at Mass

We may use any prayers that we wish and that help us most, but it is generally admitted that it is best to use a prayerbook and follow, as closely as we can, the Mass with the priest.

The Confiteor. When the priest bends down at the beginning of the Mass and says the *Confiteor,* we, too, should unite ourselves with Jesus in His Agony, should humbly confess our faults and ask pardon for them through the merits of Christ's agony.

We then follow the various prayers with the celebrant.

At the Sanctus we should remember that the Angels come down to assist at Mass in multitudes and that we are in the midst of them, and we should join our voices with theirs in adoring and praising God. They present our prayers to God.

At the Consecration we should be filled with the deepest reverence and love, for Jesus is really born in the hands of the priest, as He was born in Bethlehem. When the priest lifts up the Sacred Host, we should look on our God in an ecstasy of joy, as the Angels look on Him in Heaven, and say, "My Lord and my God."

At the Consecration of the Precious Blood we must remember that all the Precious Blood that Jesus shed on Calvary is in the Chalice, and we should offer it to God with the priest for God's glory and for our own intentions.

It is well to place ourselves, our sins, all our intentions, our dear ones, the souls in Purgatory in all the chalices being at this moment offered to God in every part of the world.

We must be full of holy awe and love from the Consecration to the Communion. We are in the midst of countless adoring Angels.

It is indeed a sign of woeful ignorance to manifest irreverence, to look around or speak during this most sacred time. It is much worse to leave the church, to abandon God dying on the altar for us. [See footnote on p. 8.] Nothing but the gravest necessity should induce one to go away until, at least, the Communion of the Priest.

Remember, Dear Reader, that the day you hear Mass is worth a thousand days to you, that all the labors and works of a day, or a week, or a whole year are nothing in comparison with the value of one Mass.

A Word to Fathers and Mothers

Reading these wonderful words of the Saints and Doctors of the Church, how is it possible that any Christian father or mother does not ardently desire to see at least one of their sons a priest.

Parents earnestly seek the welfare of their children; they strive to procure for them every happiness, every benefit, every honor.

How lamentable, then, is it that they so rarely seek for them the greatest of all honors, viz., the priesthood.

It is true we have heard of some families which count as many as three, four, six sons as priests, but alas, these are very few!